Abductions

by Katie Chanez

raintree

Raintree is an imprint of Capstone Global Library Limited, a company incorporated in England and Wales having its registered office at 264 Banbury Road, Oxford, OX2 7DY – Registered company number: 6695582

www.raintree.co.uk
myorders@raintree.co.uk

Edited by Claire Vanden Branden
Designed by Becky Daum
Original illustrations © Capstone Global Library Limited 2020
Production by Melissa Martin
Originated by Capstone Global Library Ltd
Printed and bound in India

978 1 4747 8750 5 (hardback)
978 1 4747 8754 3 (paperback)

British Library Cataloguing in Publication Data
A full catalogue record for this book is available from the British Library.

Acknowledgements
We would like to thank the following for permission to reproduce photographs: Alamy: AF archive/Paramount Pictures, 15, World History Archive, 9; iStockphoto: AntonioGuillem, 22–23, cosmin4000, 11, 28, goktugg, 31, gremlin, 24–25, Magnilion, 16–17, Mike_Kiev, cover, patrickheagney, 6–7; Shutterstock Images: Fer Gregory, 21, ktsdesign, 5, lassedesignen, 26–27, Linda Bucklin, 18–19, 29, vchal, 12–13. Design elements: Shutterstock Images, Red Line Editorial.

CONTENTS

CHAPTER 1

TAKEN

Barney and Betty Hill were driving home in 1961. They had been on holiday. Suddenly a light appeared above them. The light seemed to chase their car. They kept driving. But the light kept following. Then they both fell asleep.

Barney and Betty woke up. They were many kilometres away. They could not remember how they got there.

Barney and Betty Hill said they were taken by aliens on 19 September 1961. Could it really have happened?

People who are under hypnosis go into a trance. Many believe hypnosis can help access memories deep in their brains.

Betty started having dreams about that night. She dreamed aliens had stopped their car. The aliens had taken them onto their spaceship. She could not get this out of her mind.

The Hills decided to see a doctor. The doctor suggested **hypnosis** to help them to remember what had happened.

The Hills decided to try it. Afterwards they said aliens had **abducted** them. They believed aliens had studied them and then made Betty and Barney forget what had happened.

THE UFO INCIDENT

A film was made in 1975 about Barney and Betty's abduction. It was called *The UFO Incident*. Reports of alien abductions rose after the film was shown.

The Hills told many people their story.

CHAPTER 2

WHO ARE the Aliens?

Betty said the aliens had grey skin. They had big eyes. They also had small ears and noses. They were about 1.5 metres (5 feet) tall. Barney said they wore black clothes. Many believers call these aliens "Greys".

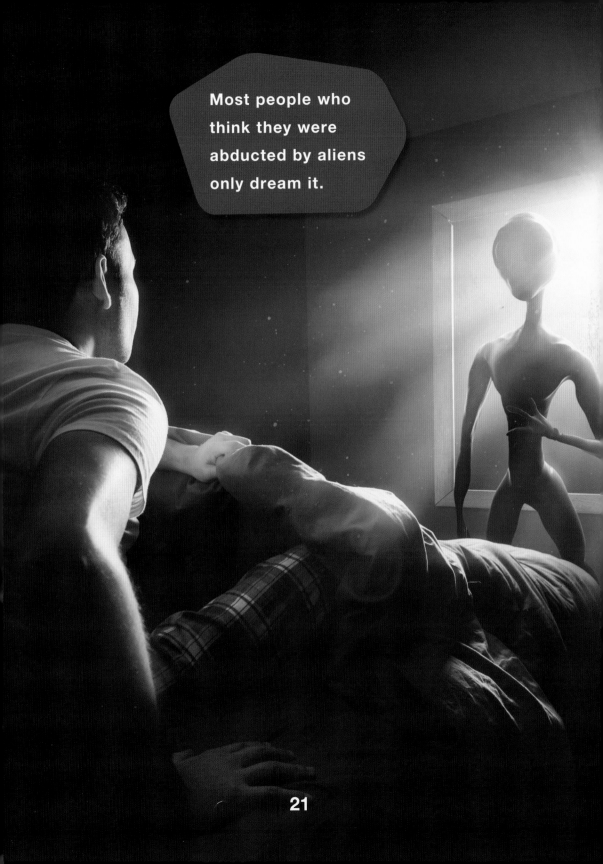

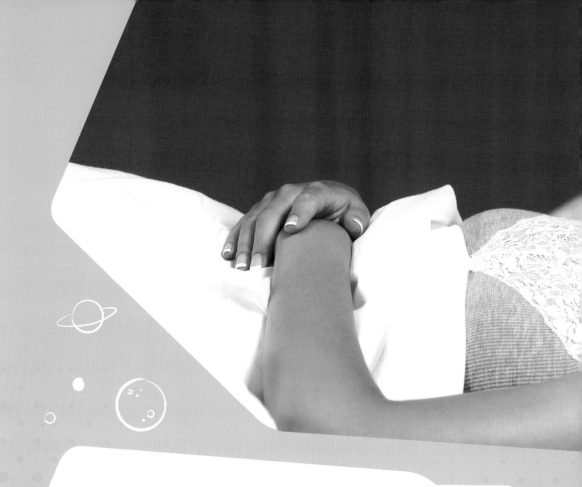

Your body relaxes when you fall
asleep. Sometimes people wake up
suddenly. They cannot move straight
away. It can be scary. Sometimes people
think they see things that are not there.
They are still dreaming.

When a person wakes up and cannot move it is called sleep paralysis.

Many people who say they were taken do not remember it at first. People can remember things differently. **Hypnotists** can accidentally make people believe things. Sometimes people remember things that never happened.

GREYS ON TELEVISION

Many TV series and films show the Greys. One TV series was on almost two weeks before Barney used hypnosis. Some people think he remembered the TV series.

Hypnosis can sometimes make people think they saw things that were never there.

Most scientists think people have only imagined that they were taken by aliens.

Many people say aliens have taken them. Most scientists think there are other explanations. Believers think scientists are ignoring the truth.

GLOSSARY

abduct
take a person by force

hypnosis
process of putting someone
into a trance

hypnotist
person who puts someone
else under hypnosis

shapeshifter
person or creature that can
change its physical form
or shape

TRIVIA

1. Betty Hill said the Greys showed her a star map, which she later drew.

2. Some people believe that government officials from around the world are secretly Reptilians, also called lizard people. They think Reptilians want to take over the world.

3. About 6 million people in the United States have reported being abducted by aliens.

ACTIVITY

CREATE YOUR OWN ALIENS!

Think about the different types of aliens mentioned in the book. Now come up with your own aliens. Where are they from? Do they abduct people? Why? What do they hope to do or learn? You can write a story from the point of view of the alien or the human. You could write one side of the story and get a friend to write another.

FIND OUT MORE

Books

Aliens and UFOs (Solving Mysteries with Science), Lori Hile (Raintree, 2013)

Can You Survive an Alien Invasion? (You Choose: Doomsday), Blake Hoena (Raintree, 2015)

Have Aliens Visited Earth? (Top Secret!), Nick Hunter (Raintree, 2017)

Paranormal Handbook to UFOs, Crop Circles and Alien Encounters, Sean McCollum (Raintree, 2016)

Website

Do aliens really exist?
www.bbc.co.uk/newsround/19840847

INDEX